Mary

Help in Hard Times

Written and compiled by
Marianne Lorraine Trouvé, FSP

Pauline
BOOKS & MEDIA
Boston

Library of Congress Cataloging-in-Publication Data

Trouvé, Marianne Lorraine.
  Mary : help in hard times / written and compiled by Marianne Lorraine Trouvé, FSP.
    pages cm
  ISBN-13: 978-0-8198-4939-7
  ISBN-10: 0-8198-4939-1
  1. Mary, Blessed Virgin, Saint. 2. Catholic Church--Doctrines. I. Title.
  BT603.T76 2014
  232.91--dc23

2013037990

The Scripture quotations contained herein are from the *New Revised Standard Version Bible: Catholic Edition,* copyright © 1989, 1993, Division of Christian Education of the National Council of the Churches of Christ in the United States of America. Used by permission. All rights reserved.

The English translation of Pope Francis's prayer to Mary, Untier of Knots, copyright © Libreria Editrice Vaticana. Used with permission.

Cover design by Rosana Usselmann

Cover art: Detail of the Virgin Mary by G. Reni

Published by Pauline Books & Media, 50 Saint Pauls Avenue, Boston, MA 02130-3491

Printed in the U.S.A.

www.pauline.org

Pauline Books & Media is the publishing house of the Daughters of St. Paul, an international congregation of women religious serving the Church with the communications media.

1 2 3 4 5 6 7 8 9   18 17 16 15 14

Contents

Introduction

What difference can Mary make in our lives of faith?

Who is Mary, and how can she still help us today?

Why is it that after Jesus himself, Mary is probably the one figure in our Catholic tradition who stands out the most? She was a young Jewish maiden who lived in an obscure village, in a remote area whose people had heard the tramp of Roman boots and who had been forced to pay taxes to Caesar. Yet, in this unlikely place, God chose to come to the earth, to take on flesh and become one of us in order to be our Redeemer, our Savior. And he chose to do this with Mary's willing, loving cooperation. When the angel whispered God's invitation in her ear, Mary said yes and never took it back. She kept on repeating it even to the day she stood under the cross, even as she saw the blood of

Jesus flowing from his wounds. In that moment, Mary became the intercessor and mother for the whole human race.

Since then, Catholics and other Christians have held Mary in a unique place of honor. Her journey of faith is a model for our own. Through the Communion of Saints, as members of the one Body of Christ, she still helps us now. It's as if every time we ask her help, the curtain between earth and heaven is drawn back and blessings flow more abundantly, like a vast waterfall of grace.

This book is about making Mary more a part of our life of faith. If you already have devotion to her, it can grow; and if until now you have not had such devotion, this is an invitation to explore it. Mary is always ready to help us, to intercede for us, and to obtain graces for us from God. In 1830, she appeared to Saint Catherine Labouré in a convent in Paris, France. As Mary held out her hands in supplication for the world, Catherine saw streams of light as bright as sunbeams flowing from beautiful rings on Mary's fingers. Mary told her, "These rays symbolize the graces I obtain for all those who ask for them." But not all the rings gave light. Mary explained, "The gems from which rays do not fall symbolize the graces that people forget to ask for." If we want to receive graces and obtain favors through Mary's intercession, all we need do is ask.

Mary is our model of faith, and the key moments of her life are like milestones in which we can also see our own history. Pope Benedict XVI spoke of this in a homily he gave on the feast of the Assumption.* The Pope noted four moments in particular: Mary's Immaculate Conception, the Annunciation, her divine Motherhood, and her Assumption. He said that Mary's Immaculate Conception points us back to God's original plan of creation, when man and woman were filled with grace and lived in loving union with God. Their sin jeopardized this plan but did not destroy it. At the Annunciation, Mary consented to God's plan, and this brought about the Incarnation of the Son of God. Thus Mary became the Mother of God. Finally, Mary's Assumption shows us the ultimate goal of our earthly journey: eternal life through Christ our Lord.

The first four chapters of this book follow the outline of Pope Benedict XVI, starting with Mary's Immaculate Conception. Looking at Mary through

---

* See Pope Benedict XVI, Homily, August 15, 2009, http://www.vatican.va/holy_father/benedict_xvi/homilies/2009/documents/hf_ben-xvi_hom_20090815_assunzione_en.html.

the lens of these four moments is a way to read our own story of faith. It's also a way of reviewing the main teaching of the Catholic faith about Mary, and of seeing how she is always so much a part of our lives. The book then offers real-life stories of how some people have experienced Mary's intercession and help in their lives, followed by a section of prayers and devotions.

Mary, Helper of the Sick

*"If you only knew how good the Blessed Virgin is!
If people only knew!"*

Saint Bernadette

Our Lady of Lourdes and the Immaculate Conception

High in the Pyrenees, the ice-cold water of the river Gave rushed along on the morning of February 11, 1858. Fourteen-year-old Bernadette had stopped to take off her stockings before wading across. Her younger sister, nine-year-old Toinette, and their friend Marie Abadie had already waded across the river. The three girls were collecting branches for firewood.

Bernadette suddenly heard a strong wind whistling through the nearby grotto, carved out of a huge rock formation. The shrubs swayed in the wind, including the delicate roses that graced the grotto. Looking up, Bernadette could hardly believe her eyes.

Standing before her, high in the grotto, was a beautiful young woman wearing a white robe with a blue sash and a long white veil. Rosary beads hung from her right arm and yellow roses rested on her feet.

Bernadette rubbed her eyes in disbelief. But when she looked up again, the lady was still there. Not knowing what to do, Bernadette pulled out her rosary beads and began to pray. The lady followed the prayers, but joined in only for the Glory Be. After the prayers, the lady disappeared.

Still in awe, Bernadette told Toinette what had happened but made her promise to keep it a secret. However, it wasn't long before Toinette told their mother, who thought it was all nonsense. She forbade Bernadette to go back to the grotto. But nothing could keep her away, and on February 14 she saw the lady again. The lady still said nothing about who she was. On February 18 the lady appeared for the third time, and she asked Bernadette to come every day for two weeks.

In the meantime, word had gotten out and crowds began to go to the grotto as well. They had concluded that the Blessed Virgin Mary was the one appearing to Bernadette, but she had never said that. In referring to the lady she used only the word "aquero," which means "that."

During the vision on February 24, the lady said, "Penance! Penance! Penance! Pray to God for sinners!" The next day, February 25, a crucial event occurred. The lady told Bernadette, "Go and drink at the spring and wash yourself in it." Bernadette was confused because there was no spring there, only the nearby river. When Bernadette went toward the river, the lady called her back. It wasn't the right place. Bernadette began to dig in the ground near where the lady had indicated. She found only mud. Three times she threw away the muddy mess. Finally, on her fourth attempt, she started to see a little bit of water trickling out of the ground. The people, meanwhile, thought she was crazy because she had washed her face with the mud. Although it was only a trickle at first, by the next day it could be clearly seen that a spring had begun to flow. There had never been one there before.

The visions continued for two weeks as the lady had promised. And after that, she appeared once more, for a total of eighteen apparitions.

On March 25, Bernadette finally asked the lady who she was. The lady looked up to heaven and said, "I am the Immaculate Conception." Bernadette didn't know what that meant, because she had not had much schooling. Trying her best to remember the words, she went and told the parish priest, Father Peyramale. He was astounded, for a little over three years earlier, on December 8, 1854, Pope Pius IX had declared the dogma of the Immaculate

Conception of Mary. So now there was no doubt that the beautiful young woman was indeed Mary, the Mother of God.

Events moved quickly after that. Mary had requested that a chapel be built there, and it was. Miraculous healings and cures had begun to occur. Larger and larger crowds flocked to Lourdes, which today is still one of the best-loved shrines in the Catholic world.

As for Bernadette, she later entered the convent, becoming a Sister of Charity at Nevers, France. In her short life—she died at thirty-five from tuberculosis—she had to endure many trials, such as poverty, illness, and misunderstanding. Mary had told her: "I do not promise to make you happy in this life, but in the next." Bernadette was canonized by Pope Pius XI on December 8, 1933, the feast of the Immaculate Conception.

The apparition of Mary to Saint Bernadette is one of the most famous accounts of how Mary has helped people. The story of Lourdes offers us many points for reflection.

Mary picks the lowly ones

Bernadette was considered a "nobody" in Lourdes, just another girl in the town. No one paid any attention to her. But Mary chose Bernadette as the one to bear her message. Mary didn't appear to the priest or any of the civil officials in the town, those who would have been thought of as "important." No, Mary looks on the lowly ones. In this, she is really only imitating God, who had chosen her. For in her own time Mary, too, was one of the lowly ones.

In her beautiful song of praise, the Magnificat, she praised God for this:

> And Mary said, "My soul magnifies the Lord,
> and my spirit rejoices in God my Savior,
> for he has looked with favor on the lowliness of his
>   servant.
> Surely, from now on all generations will call me
>   blessed;
> for the Mighty One has done great things
>   for me,
> and holy is his name.
> His mercy is for those who fear him
> from generation to generation.
> He has shown strength with his arm;
> he has scattered the proud in the thoughts of their
>   hearts.
> He has brought down the powerful from their
>   thrones,
> and lifted up the lowly; he has filled the hungry
>   with good things,
> and sent the rich away empty." (Lk 1:46–53)

This is good news for us, too, because most of us are not counted among the mighty ones of the world. But we are extremely important in the eyes of God, for each one of us is made in God's image and likeness. This gives us great confidence in approaching God through our tender mother Mary.

Mary asked not only for prayer but for penance

It's very striking that Mary repeated three times, "Penance! Penance! Penance!" The first apparition, on February 11, took place one week before Lent started that year. Most of the remaining apparitions to Bernadette happened during Lent. So we can see a certain connection between Lourdes and Lent, one that goes far beyond wearing ashes on our foreheads.

Traditionally, the three most common works of penance during Lent are prayer, fasting, and almsgiving. This last one can be thought of in a wider sense than that of simply making monetary offerings, though that has its place. Almsgiving can mean doing works of mercy, such as feeding the hungry or giving clothes to the needy.

Penance can certainly help us get our own lives in order. It can help us to be more disciplined and so become more spiritually fruitful in our lives. But it can also help others, and this is what Mary was speaking about. She not only asked for penance, but told us to pray to God for sinners. In some mysterious way, because we are members of Christ's Mystical Body, the Church, we can help sinners when we pray and offer penance for them. Saint Paul wrote, "I am now rejoicing in my sufferings for your sake, and in my flesh I am completing what is lacking in Christ's afflictions for the sake of his body, that is, the church" (Col 1:24). So our sufferings don't go to waste, because God can use them when we join them to the sufferings of Jesus Christ.

Mary brings healing and peace

Lourdes has become famous as a shrine for healing, where physical diseases have been cured in a miraculous way. So far the Church has officially approved sixty-seven of these miracles, which have gone through a very rigorous process to ascertain their authenticity. But many thousands of pilgrims have been helped physically, emotionally, and spiritually by their prayers to Our Lady offered in faith. Mary obtains these graces for us through her intercession.

We don't have to go to Lourdes in order to experience Mary's loving care for us. All we need do is turn to her in prayer and ask for her help. This can be as simple as spontaneously saying, "Mary, help me!" when a need arises, or it can mean praying the Rosary or meditating on Mary's example in the Gospels. (A later section of stories recounts some ways in which various people have turned to Mary for help). Just as any loving mother will rush to the side of her child who has fallen and scraped her knee, Mary will rush to our side as we pray and bring our petitions to Jesus, her Son.

The Immaculate Conception

The story of Bernadette and Lourdes is closely connected to the Immaculate Conception, a Marian feast the Church celebrates every year on December 8. But what does that teaching mean? First, let's clear away a common misunderstanding. It's not to be confused with the Virgin Birth, which means that Mary conceived and gave birth to Jesus while remaining a virgin. Instead, the Immaculate Conception means that Mary herself was free from original sin from the very first moment she was conceived (in the normal way by her mother Saint Anne). Her soul was filled with grace.

Original sin is the burden of sin that we all carry as members of a fallen race. It is not any personal sin that we commit. It means that we are born into the world without the gift of sanctifying grace that makes us holy. The *Catechism of the Catholic Church* explains:

> Still, the transmission of original sin is a mystery that we cannot fully understand. But we do know by Revelation that Adam had received original holiness and justice not for himself alone, but for all human nature. By yielding to the tempter, Adam and Eve committed a personal sin, but this sin affected the human nature that they would then transmit in a fallen state. It is a sin which will be transmitted by propagation to all mankind, that is, by the transmission of a human nature deprived of original holiness and justice. And that is why original sin is called "sin" only in an analogical sense: it is a sin "contracted" and not "committed"—a state and not an act. (CCC, no. 404)

By God's grace Mary was preserved from this sinful state, in view of her special mission to be the Mother of God. She received this grace through the merits of Jesus, by his suffering, death, and resurrection. So she was redeemed, too, but in a different way. "In order for Mary to be able to give the free assent of her faith to the announcement of her vocation, it was necessary that she be wholly borne by God's grace." (CCC, no. 490)

In other words, Mary was completely dependent on God, who gave her the gift of holiness. God's grace enabled her to cooperate with the divine plan of salvation. So what does this mean for our life? It reminds us that through our Baptism we have been freed from original sin and restored to God's friendship through grace. Should we have the misfortune to fall into sin again, we have access to grace and forgiveness through the sacrament of Reconciliation. One day we, too, will be free of all sin when we reach eternal life in heaven. Our task on our earthly journey is to turn away from sin now, to make it less a part of our life. As long as we are on earth we will never be completely free of it. But aided by God's grace, we can make good choices today, right now, choices that will lead us closer to God and away from sin. In doing this, we can turn to Mary for help. Precisely because she was free of sin, she is compassionate and loving. She understands the trials we face and the difficulties we must go through in life. And she is right there by our side, walking with us to encourage us when we feel like we want to quit. Mary will never let us down.

For Reflection and Prayer

1. Mary makes clear that God looks with favor on the lowly ones of the world. Yet the values of the world tend to focus on notoriety, success, and money. In your own life, how do you find a balance between the values of the Gospel and the need to make a living?

2. Why do you think that Mary asked for penance? What are some ways that you can practice penance in your daily life?

3. A highlight of any pilgrimage to Lourdes is going to the baths at the spring. This immersion in water can recall our Baptism, which takes away all sins. Take some time to renew your baptismal commitment, perhaps the next time you go to confession. If you have ever visited Lourdes, what impressed you most?

Cause of Our Joy

"And why has this happened to me, that the mother of my Lord comes to me? For as soon as I heard the sound of your greeting, the child in my womb leaped for joy" (Lk 1:43–44).

Words of Elizabeth to Mary

Mary, the Virgin-Mother Who Brings Us Joy

It would be a truism to say that everybody wants to be happy. Who doesn't desire happiness? Yet at times it is so hard to find. As the Book of Lamentations puts it, "My soul is bereft of peace; I have forgotten what happiness is" (3:17).

One of the titles of Mary is "Cause of Our Joy." Why do we call her that? How does Mary bring us joy? A good place to begin is to re-read the beautiful Gospel account of the Annunciation to Mary:

> In the sixth month the angel Gabriel was sent by God to a town in Galilee called Nazareth, to a virgin engaged to a man whose name was Joseph, of the house of David. The virgin's name was Mary. And he came to her and said, "Greetings, favored one! The Lord is with you." But she was much perplexed by his words and pondered what sort of greeting this might be. The angel said to her, "Do not be afraid, Mary, for you have found favor with God. And now, you will

conceive in your womb and bear a son, and you will name him Jesus. He will be great, and will be called the Son of the Most High, and the Lord God will give to him the throne of his ancestor David. He will reign over the house of Jacob forever, and of his kingdom there will be no end." Mary said to the angel, "How can this be, since I am a virgin?" The angel said to her, "The Holy Spirit will come upon you, and the power of the Most High will overshadow you; therefore the child to be born will be holy; he will be called Son of God. And now, your relative Elizabeth in her old age has also conceived a son; and this is the sixth month for her who was said to be barren. For nothing will be impossible with God." Then Mary said, "Here am I, the servant of the Lord; let it be with me according to your word." Then the angel departed from her. (Lk 1:26–38)

When Gabriel greets Mary, he tells her to rejoice. "Greetings," used in the translation above, doesn't express the wonderful richness of the actual Greek word, *chaire*, which literally means "rejoice!" The angel is bringing Mary good news, which will make her happy. God has chosen her for a special mission—so special, in fact, that it is completely unique in the history of the human race. God asked Mary to become the mother of his own Son.

But notice that even before the angel gets to that part, he tells Mary to rejoice because "the Lord is with you." God was already present in Mary through grace, which is a wonderful reason to rejoice. Through the gift of grace, the Holy Trinity, Father, Son, and Holy Spirit, was already dwelling in Mary's soul.

Yet the news would get even better. God was proposing an invitation to Mary. He was asking her to become the mother of his Son. God wanted to take on flesh and become a man—if Mary would agree to accept this important role of motherhood. Mary only had one question: How would it happen since, as she said, "I know not man"?

Gabriel told her that the Holy Spirit would overshadow her and bring about this conception in a miraculous way—Mary would remain a virgin—because the holy child to be born would be the Son of God. Gabriel's words were enough for Mary. Immediately she accepted God's invitation: "Here am I, the servant of the Lord; let it be with me according to your word." And the Incarnation happened.

Mary shows us how to have a happy life

How do we know that Mary accepted God's invitation with joy? We can say this because the word used in the Gospel (*genoito*) indicates it. Scripture scholars tell us that this word is in a form that expresses a desire, in fact an ardent desire or a joyful willingness to take on a task.* The entire account of the Annunciation, from the opening word "Rejoice!" to Mary's joyful acceptance is filled with a spirit of joy and happiness.

What stands out most in the Annunciation is how willing Mary was to make a gift of herself to God. She offered herself with joy, and this meant specifically that she offered the gift of her virginity.

It's hard for us to understand how radical her gift was, because she lived in a culture where marriage was prized above all, and virginity offered to God was not an option for a young Jewish girl. So why did Mary accept so readily? It could only be because somehow the Holy Spirit gave her the light to understand. It happened because Mary had a relationship with the Holy Spirit.

What kind of relationship was it? It was rooted in the gift of grace that had been given to her even before her birth. We know that through grace the Holy Spirit dwells in us. Mary lived with the indwelling Spirit for her whole life. The Spirit cer-

---

* For details on this, see *Mary in the Mystery of the Covenant*, Ignace de la Potterie, trans. Bertrand Buby (New York: Alba House, 1992).

tainly was active in her, giving her mind light and helping her to understand the Scriptures that she, as a devout Jew, would have heard in the synagogue.

That grace bore fruit in Mary because she reflected on everything. Luke tells us twice that "Mary treasured all these words and pondered them in her heart" (Lk 2:19; see 2:51). Her habit of reflection and prayer made her open to the angel's message. In a beautiful passage, the prophet Isaiah tells us that God sends forth his word:

> "For as the rain and the snow come down from heaven,
> and do not return there until they have watered the earth,
> making it bring forth and sprout,
> giving seed to the sower and bread to the eater,
> so shall my word be that goes out from my mouth;
> it shall not return to me empty,
> but it shall accomplish that which I purpose,
> and succeed in the thing for which I sent it."
> (Is 55:10–11)

God's word "succeeded" in Mary because she completely opened herself to it. And the gift of her virginity was the fruit of her relationship with the Holy Spirit.

Mary was full of joy

Joy is one of the fruits of the Spirit: "The fruit of the Spirit is love, joy . . ." (Gal 5:22). So we can be sure that Mary, being so open to the Spirit, was full of joy. And Mary was free from sin, the source of sadness. Saint Thomas reminds us: "Sadness, as an evil or vice, is caused by a disordered love for oneself, which . . . is the general root of all vices" (*Summa Theol.*, II-II, q. 28, a. 4, ad 1; see I-II, q. 72, a. 4). Notice that Saint Thomas isn't saying that love for oneself is wrong, but a *disordered* love for oneself is. That's the kind of love that makes us seek our own good at the expense of others.

Mary wasn't like that at all. The Gospel of Luke goes on to tell us that once Mary had heard from the Angel Gabriel that Elizabeth was in need, Mary hurried to help her, putting her cousin's needs ahead of her own. And when she visited her relatives, she brought joy not only to Elizabeth but also to the baby in her womb:

> In those days Mary set out and went with haste to a Judean town in the hill country, where she entered the house of Zechariah and greeted Elizabeth. When Elizabeth heard Mary's greeting, the child leaped in her womb. And Elizabeth was filled with the Holy Spirit and exclaimed

with a loud cry, "Blessed are you among women, and blessed is the fruit of your womb. And why has this happened to me, that the mother of my Lord comes to me? For as soon as I heard the sound of your greeting, the child in my womb leaped for joy." (Lk 1:39–44)

John leaped in the womb; he danced for joy at the sound of Mary's voice. She bore within her the presence of the unborn Christ as the source of joy. John was destined to be a prophet, also filled with the Holy Spirit. This beautiful scene of the Visitation tells us that somehow Mary's fullness of grace, along with the joy it brought her, can be communicated to others. Her voice was like a spark that ignited a fire in John, and that fire would burn in his prophetic words calling the people to repentance. The fire had its source in the Holy Spirit, of course, but Mary was the kindling that the Holy Spirit used.

Just as she did for John, Mary can kindle in us the fire of God's love and the dance of joy. Mary shows us that doing God's will is not drudgery or, worse yet, an enslavement. Instead, it is the breath of fresh air that lifts us up and carries us along so that we can fly straight to God: "Those who wait for the LORD shall renew their strength, they shall mount up with wings like eagles, they shall run and not be weary, they shall walk and not faint" (Is 40:31).

Mary's gift of self

As the Virgin-Mother, Mary made a spousal gift of herself to God in a virginal way. In other words, while remaining a virgin, she offered herself to God to fully cooperate in his plan of salvation. For her, this involved becoming the mother of Jesus, our Savior. We live in a culture where so many people have been shell-shocked by the sexual revolution. It's hard to escape its effects, just as it's hard to escape the fallout from a nuclear explosion. So people may find it hard to understand why God wanted Mary to be a virgin. The reason for Mary's virginity was not to somehow give the impression that sex is bad, but to safeguard the mystery of Christ. As the *Catechism* tells us: "Mary's virginity manifests God's absolute initiative in the Incarnation. Jesus has only God as Father" (no. 503). The humanity of Jesus was drawn from that of Mary, but the fact that he has no human father underscores his divinity.

What lesson can we draw for our own lives? Mary teaches us that the way to be happy is to make a joyful gift of ourselves to God and to others. The details of how we do that are different for each person. God calls each of us to our own unique vocation. Most people live out this vocation in the beauty of marriage and family life. God calls others to a form of consecrated life, to continence "for the sake of the kingdom." Whatever our vocation, we will find happiness to the degree that we make a gift of ourselves to others. Then we, too, can joyfully say with Mary, "Here am I, the servant of the Lord; let it be with me according to your word."

For Reflection and Prayer

1. Joy is one of the fruits of the Holy Spirit. What are some ways you might cultivate a deeper awareness of God's presence and of the way the Holy Spirit dwells in us through grace, bringing joy?

2. Sin promises joy but doesn't deliver on that promise. If you are struggling with some area of sin in your life, bring it in prayer to Mary and ask her to help you.

3. Prayerfully re-read Luke's account of the Annunciation and consider how Mary made a joyful gift of herself. How might you make a gift of yourself in your life, to God, and to the people you love?

"Am I Not Your Mother?"

"Are you not under my shadow and protection? . . . Is there anything else that you need?"

OUR LADY TO SAINT JUAN DIEGO

Mary Is Our Mother Too

Juan Diego was making his long trip to Mass on the cold morning of December 9, 1531, which at that time was the feast of the Immaculate Conception. Suddenly he heard some strains of beautiful music. Looking to see where it came from, Juan found himself at the top of Tepeyac Hill, near Mexico City. He was startled to see a beautiful young woman standing there. She looked like a morena, that is, one of his own people. In his own language, Nahuatl, she called him by name, using a nickname that showed great affection: "Juanito," she said, "Juan Dieguito, where are you going?"

Hardly knowing what to make of it all, Juan's words tumbled out, "I am on my way to Mass." As if to answer his unspoken question, the lady continued, "Know and understand, dearest of my children, that I am the ever-holy Virgin Mary, Mother of the true God who gives life, Mother of the Creator of heaven and earth."

Mary, the Mother of God? Juan thought. *How is it possible that she should come to me? Who am I? I am no one of importance!* Despite his own estimation of him-self, the Virgin Mary entrusted him with a great task. She told Juan that she wanted a church to be built there on that spot. Why? Mary herself told him that she wanted to "show forth all my love, compassion, assistance, and defense because I am your loving Mother: yours, and all who are with you, and of all who live in this land, and of all who love me, call to me, and trust in me. I will hear their cries and will give remedy to their sor-rows and sufferings."

Then the beautiful Lady told Juan to bring her message to the bishop. Juan did as she asked. But the bishop, Juan de Zumárraga, was skeptical that the Blessed Virgin Mary had really appeared to the humble man before him. Though he spoke kindly to Juan Diego, he was not convinced.

Downhearted, Juan Diego left the bishop's resi-dence. He again saw the Lady when he passed by Tepeyac and in dismay reported that he had not succeeded.

But the Lady, not to be daunted, repeated her commission. Juan Diego *had* to go back to the bishop. So he did. After being made to wait a long time, he was finally allowed to see the bishop again, who asked Juan to bring him back some sign so that he could know for certain that the Blessed Virgin

Mary had appeared to him. So Juan went back home, wondering where all this would lead.

In the meantime, however, his uncle had fallen sick. Juan was in a hurry to go and get a priest to bring him the sacraments, so he tried to avoid seeing the Lady. He took a detour. But the Lady appeared to him anyway. Calling him "my little son," she asked him where he was going. When he told her, the Lady reassured him that his uncle would recover. With a look of great love, Mary smiled at him and gently chided him for his doubts, *"Do not let anything afflict you, and do not be afraid of any illness, or accident, or pain. Am I not here who am your Mother? Are you not under my shadow and protection? Do you need anything else?"*

After those comforting words, Mary told Juan to gather the flowers he would find at the top of the hill and bring them to her. *Flowers in December?* he wondered, but he obediently did as she asked. When he arrived at the top of the hill, he couldn't believe what he saw: beautiful Castilian roses at the peak of their bloom! He gathered as many as he could hold and brought them to the Lady, who lovingly arranged them in his tilma. She then told him to bring them to the bishop.

When he returned to the bishop's residence, he again had to wait but finally was able to meet the bishop. When Juan opened his cloak and the beautiful roses spilled out, the bishop and others in the room were astounded at what they saw: an image of the Lady imprinted on Juan's tilma. This image, of course, is the amazing icon of Our Lady of Guadalupe, patron of Mexico and loving Mother of all people.

The beautiful story of Our Lady of Guadalupe is a vivid, touching reminder of how much Mary cares about us and wants to help us in our needs. It offers us much to reflect on. Here are a few points that we can apply to our own lives.

Mary called Juan Diego by name

Not only did Mary call Juan Diego by name, but she used an affectionate term, almost a nickname, "Juanito . . . Juan Dieguito." This shows us how tender and loving Mary is, that she not only knows each of our names but also our nicknames as well. This tells us that we can approach her with great confidence and love.

In the Bible, knowing someone's name means to really know that person. The Book of Revelation says, "Let anyone who has an ear listen to what the Spirit is saying to the churches. To everyone who conquers I will give some of the hidden manna, and

I will give a white stone, and on the white stone is written a new name that no one knows except the one who receives it" (Rev 2:17).

Isn't it beautiful to think that God has given each of us a special name, one that no one else knows except God and ourselves? And while this passage doesn't specifically mention Mary, it is reasonable to think that Mary knows our special name too. This name expresses who we really are and what we are called to do. In calling us by our special name of grace, Mary will lead us to her Son, Jesus, who will fill us with graces and blessings.

Mary spoke Juan's language

Mary spoke to Juan Diego in his own dialect. In fact, this also occurred at other Marian apparitions. When she appeared to Saint Bernadette at Lourdes, for example, Mary did not speak in French but in the local dialect. At Guadalupe, Mary not only spoke the native language but her appearance also reflected the native features, as did the way she was dressed. Mary comes to us in a way that we can understand. So when we approach Mary in prayer, we can come to her just as we are. We don't need to put on any pretenses. If we're down and out, we can tell her that. If we feel weighed down by sin, we can tell her that too. Whatever our condition, we can simply go to Mary and she will help us.

Once at a conference I heard an amazing testimony from a man who had converted from an extremely sinful lifestyle and had lived far from God. As a fallen-away Catholic, he had been very promiscuous, even to the point of acting in pornographic films. When the films began to involve blasphemy and sacrilege, such as desecrating the crucifix and other sacred objects, he went along with it. But he started to feel revulsion at this and wanted to change. One day, not knowing where to turn, he came across a rosary. He still remembered how to pray it, so he started to do so, one Hail Mary at a time. That was the beginning of an amazing conversion. It took time and the way had its ups and downs, but that one Hail Mary was the first step on his road back to God. He said that Mary "cleaned him up." So no matter what state you find yourself in, don't be afraid to turn to Mary for help. She will not let you down! Our journey back to God can begin even with one Hail Mary.

Mary asked for a church to be built in her honor

Why did Mary ask for a church? It wasn't for her own benefit. Instead, she wanted it to be a place where people could come so that she could fully be a mother to *all* the people. She wanted to console, help, and remedy their afflictions, not only individually, but also for the people as a whole.

We live in an individualistic age, and that is at least part of the reason why many people have stopped going to church. Although the statistics vary from place to place, Mass attendance among Catholics has fallen off dramatically since the 1960s. In some areas, less than 20 percent of Catholics participate in Mass every Sunday. That could only happen when people lose the sense of worshipping God as a community. We come together to worship because God is present not only in us individually through grace, but also in the church community as a whole.

We can't offer the Eucharist on our own. So by asking for a church to be built, Mary was telling us that it is important to come to church for prayer, especially for the Eucharist. The great Marian shrines around the world, including that of Guadalupe, are also known for devotion to the Holy Eucharist, both in the Mass itself and through adoration. Again, we can see that Mary's role is always to bring us closer to Jesus, her Son.

Mary Is the Mother of God

What does it mean to say that Mary is the Mother of God? This is the basic reality about Mary, the most fundamental truth about her from which everything else flows.

First, to clarify this, let's consider what it *doesn't* mean. It doesn't mean that Mary is divine or some sort of super-human being. No, she is one of us. She is not the mother of divinity itself. She is a creature like us. She was created by God, but given unique gifts in view of her special mission. We can say that Mary is the Mother of God because she is the mother of Jesus Christ, who is both God and man.

To further unpack this, let's go back—*way back*—to the fifth century. Christians had long been used to honoring Mary with the title "Mother of God." The Angel Gabriel had told her, "The Holy Spirit will come upon you, and the power of the Most High will overshadow you; therefore the child to be born will be holy; he will be called Son of God" (Lk 1:35). So devotion had sprung up in the Church to Mary as the Mother of God. It seemed straightforward: Mary was the Mother of Jesus, who is God, so she is the Mother of God.

But then a bishop named Nestorius, the patriarch of Constantinople, started to preach that people should not call Mary the Mother of God, but only the Mother of Christ. Nestorius was trying to preserve the truth that Jesus is both God and man, fully divine and fully human. But Nestorius went too far, and in effect he split Jesus into two separate persons. He made humanity and divinity in Jesus so far apart that what Jesus did as man was not a divine action, which meant that his suffering and death couldn't redeem us. And, said Nestorius, since Mary was the mother of the human Jesus, we can't call her Mother of God.

Saint Cyril, the bishop of Alexandria in Egypt, reacted strongly to this false teaching. He explained with great theological depth and clarity that Jesus has two natures, divine and human. And those natures are united in only one Person—the second Person of the Trinity. So we can indeed call Mary the Mother of God because the Person she gave birth to was the Son of God incarnate. Cyril presided at the Council of Ephesus in 431, which affirmed the truth that Mary is the Mother of God, the *Theotokos* in Greek.

Mary Leads Us to Jesus

So what is the point of all this? It shows that everything about Mary leads back to Jesus. In calling her Mother of God, in fact we are affirming the truth that Jesus is both God and man. Whatever the Catholic Church teaches about Mary is rooted in its faith in Jesus Christ. The *Catechism of the Catholic Church* states this very succinctly: "What the Catholic faith believes about Mary is based on what it believes about Christ, and what it teaches about Mary illumines in turn its faith in Christ" (no. 487).

Every teaching about Mary, whether it concerns her virginity, her Immaculate Conception, her Assumption, or her maternal mediation, is rooted in Jesus Christ and leads us to a deeper knowledge of him. Mother and Son are always found together. So we don't have to worry that if we honor Mary, we will forget about Jesus. Not at all! In fact, the great Marian shrines around the world are places of pilgrimage not just to honor Mary, but also to honor Jesus. Lourdes, for example, is famous for its Eucharistic procession, where Jesus in the Blessed Sacrament is honored and invoked.

For Reflection and Prayer

I. Prayerfully consider the quote about receiving a new name: "To everyone who conquers

I will give some of the hidden manna, and I will give a white stone, and on the white stone is written a new name that no one knows except the one who receives it" (Rev 2:17). Ask Mary to help you perceive what that name might be. Perhaps it reflects something about you as a person, or about the mission God is calling you to. For example, Jesus gave Simon the name Peter (rock), in view of his role in the Church.

2. Mary meets us where we are at. In what ways have you felt Mary's help at various times in your life? How do you respond to her words to Saint Juan Diego: Am I not here who am your Mother? Are you not under my shadow and protection? Do you need anything else?"

3. What connections do you see between Mary and the Eucharist? How can this help you deepen your appreciation and love for the Mass?

Our Heavenly Mother
and Intercessor

"It is fitting that her name is Mary, which is interpreted Star of the Sea, for just as sailors are directed to port by the star of the sea, so too Christians are directed by Mary to glory."

SAINT THOMAS AQUINAS,
Catechetical Instructions of Saint Thomas Aquinas

Mary and the Assumption

A few years ago I went to see the tall ships that were visiting Boston harbor. On my way home I stopped at Saint Anthony's Shrine downtown. As I was walking toward it, I noticed a tall, thin man hanging around in front of the church, sort of huddled into a corner wall. Though he looked around furtively through his black-rimmed glasses and seemed a bit timid, he didn't appear to be begging. True to my New York upbringing, I began to walk quickly past, pretending not to notice. As I went by, he suddenly reached into a white plastic grocery bag, pulled out a leaflet, and waved it in my face. I realized immediately that it was one of those anti-Catholic tracts, so I didn't take it.

After a short time praying in the church, I got an inspiration that on my way out I should stop and talk to this man. I felt reluctant, since I generally don't approach strangers on the street and talk to them. But I thought: *Here's this person handing out anti-Catholic leaflets in front of a Catholic church, so why should I just go by without responding in some way?* So I asked him, "What's that you're handing out?"

He handed me the leaflet, listing some typical fundamentalist objections to the Catholic Church. He said he had been Catholic but now was going to another church. His big point was that the Catholic Church has "man-made" beliefs and practices, and of course, the intercession of Mary and the saints was a huge issue. So I talked to him for a while about this. I wish I could say that he converted back to the Church, but it's never that easy. Only the grace of God can bring that about.

Why Intercession?

Perhaps, however, if Catholics had a better understanding of why we have devotion to Mary and the saints, they would not fall away so easily when challenged about this. So the question arises: Why do we ask Mary's intercession at all? Can't we just go directly to Jesus? Yes, we can and certainly do pray directly to God and to Jesus, who is the "one mediator between God and humankind" (1 Tim 2:5). In this, as in so many other things Catholic, it's not a matter or either/or, but of both/and.

Jesus came to earth for our salvation. He redeemed us by his death on the cross and his resurrection. Without that, we could not be saved. But Jesus established the Church and wanted us to play a part in helping others to be saved. For example, shortly before he went back to heaven, he told his disciples, "Go into all the world and proclaim the good news to the whole creation. The one who believes and is baptized will be saved; but the one who does not believe will be condemned" (Mk 16:15–16). Jesus gave the disciples a role through which others would be saved. Their role was subordinate to that of Jesus, of course, but it was still a true role. Something similar is at work with the intercession of Mary and the saints. It is part of the plan of God, by which he wills that we can help each other along the way of salvation.

Jesus merited for us the gift of grace, which is how we become like God. Jesus undid the evil of the original sin committed by our first parents at the very beginning of the human race. The irony is that in sinning they thought they would become like God, as the tempter told them (see Gen 3:4–5). But in reality they were already like God since he had given them the gift of original grace, and they lost it when they sinned.

So how do we become like God? The short
answer is through faith and the sacraments. Looking
at it more broadly, however, Saint Thomas makes an
interesting point. I'm paraphrasing a bit, but basically he says that we can become like God in two
ways. First, because God is good, we become like
him by being good. Second, because God is the
cause of goodness in creatures, we become like God
by bringing goodness to others, by doing good (see
Summa Theol., I, q. 103, a. 4).

That second point is the key aspect in regard to
the intercession of the saints. By praying for us, they
play a role in bringing goodness to us. It's part of
God's plan. It's more perfect for us to reflect God's
goodness by doing good rather than simply by being
good. We're meant to be active, to reach out, to help
others, and that reflects God. And while we can help
others in all sorts of ways, to help them get closer to
God is the best thing we can do for them. The intercession of the saints does precisely that.

When you think about it, isn't this the way
God acts in regard to other things? He brings
about goodness through other creatures. For
example, he could have just directly created all the
people he wanted, instead of having them come
into the world through their parents. But, by giving parents a role in procreation, God is acting

through them to bring goodness to others. And the parents' role is not only good for their children, but good for themselves too. It gives them the wonderful ability to cooperate with God in bringing life into the world.

That's good for us, because it's an important part of the way we become holy. We reflect these two aspects of God by both *being* good and *doing* good. God isn't concerned about doing things in the most efficient way. If he were, he would just do everything himself. God is concerned about drawing us into his very life, and he doesn't want us to come all by ourselves. He wants us to come with a lot of other people.

The Catholic faith takes this seriously. It's not just a matter of me and Jesus, but of me, Jesus, and the whole community of the Church. The Catholic faith is not an individualistic religion, but a communal one. And this is exactly how the Bible shows us that God acted. God chose Abraham as our father in faith, and through him built up the people of God, Israel. Throughout the Old Testament, God's dealing with Israel showed how he was concerned for the entire nation. In the New Testament, God continued this same pattern. Jesus established the Church as the new People of God. As Saint Paul says:

Now there are varieties of gifts, but the same
Spirit; and there are varieties of services, but the
same Lord; and there are varieties of activities,
but it is the same God who activates all of them
in everyone. To each is given the manifestation of
the Spirit for the common good. To one is given
through the Spirit the utterance of wisdom, and
to another the utterance of knowledge according
to the same Spirit, to another faith by the same
Spirit, to another gifts of healing by the one
Spirit, to another the working of miracles, to
another prophecy, to another the discernment of
spirits, to another various kinds of tongues, to
another the interpretation of tongues. All these
are activated by one and the same Spirit, who
allots to each one individually just as the Spirit
chooses.

For just as the body is one and has many
members, and all the members of the body,
though many, are one body, so it is with Christ.
For in the one Spirit we were all baptized into
one body—Jews or Greeks, slaves or free—and
we were all made to drink of one Spirit. Indeed,
the body does not consist of one member but of
many. . . . Now you are the body of Christ and
individually members of it. And God has
appointed in the church first apostles, second
prophets, third teachers; then deeds of power,

then gifts of healing, forms of assistance, forms of leadership, various kinds of tongues. (1 Cor 12:4–14, 27–28)

One of the "forms of assistance" is to pray and intercede for others—and we can keep on doing that once we reach heaven. Among all the saints, however, Mary has a unique role because she played a special part in the life of Jesus. By giving birth to him, she became the Mother of God. We wouldn't have Jesus if Mary had refused God's invitation. Thankfully for us, she accepted it.

On Calvary, Mary offered up her sufferings at seeing Jesus die such a cruel death. She joined her sufferings to his and so she became the Sorrowful Mother, the mother who understands our own pain and sufferings. As Jesus was dying, he saw Mary standing there with the beloved disciple. Turning toward them, Jesus said, "'Woman, here is your son.' Then [turning to John,] he said to the disciple, 'Here is your mother.' And from that hour the disciple took her into his own home" (Jn 19:26–27). Even though we usually think of Saint John as being the beloved disciple, and he probably was, he is never named in John's Gospel. Some writers think this is because he is meant to represent all of us as disciples. So in giving Mary to him, in effect Jesus was giving her to all of us. He was asking us to bring Mary into our lives, to welcome her and give her a place. It's as if Jesus was asking us to develop a relationship with Mary.

So how do we do that? Basically, we can do it just as we develop other relationships, by getting to know the person and sharing knowledge of ourselves. Granted, it may be a little harder to do this in regard to Mary, since prayer operates differently than when we speak to others face to face. And even though when we pray we may not hear a response, we can know without a doubt that she is listening to what we say and bringing it to Jesus. She will ask him for all the graces we need.

The Assumption

At the end of her life, Mary was taken into heaven in her body and soul. When we die, our soul leaves our body to appear before God, while the body decays on earth. But at the end of time, when Christ comes again in glory, our bodies will rise and be reunited to our souls (see 1 Cor 15). In Mary's case, however, God gave a special gift: her body did not remain on earth to decay, but was raised immediately to the glory of heaven. This is called the Assumption, and the Church celebrates this feast every year on August 15. A week later, on August 22, the feast of Mary's Queenship is celebrated. In reality, these two feasts are aspects of one reality. When Mary went to heaven, she took on a special role of interceding for the Church.

She had begun this role while still on earth. After Jesus ascended into heaven, Mary was with the apostles and other disciples in the Upper Room: "When they had entered the city, they went to the room upstairs where they were staying, Peter, and John, and James, and Andrew, Philip and Thomas, Bartholomew and Matthew, James son of Alphaeus, and Simon the Zealot, and Judas son of James. All these were constantly devoting themselves to prayer, together with certain women, including Mary the mother of Jesus" (Acts 1:13–14).

Knowing that Mary and the other saints are interceding for us is a great comfort and has always been an important part of the Catholic experience. (A later chapter of this book has various stories recounting graces and favors obtained through Mary's intercession.) The following story, while it does not directly deal with Mary, is a beautiful example of how the saints can help those who are at the point of death. It is a true story recounted by one of the sisters in my community, Sr. Margaret Kerry.

> When my dad was dying, the family kept vigil with him in his room for a few days. One evening Dad said he noticed someone in the room with us. He looked toward the ceiling and asked me, "Who is that?" I couldn't see anyone, so I asked him who it looked like. To my surprise, he said, "Pope John XXIII." So we started talking about John XXIII. The next morning my brother looked him up on the Internet and printed his picture.

> Shortly after, a priest we knew came to administer the Sacrament of the Sick. Knowing of Dad's illness, the priest, who had just been in Rome, had already been praying for him. We told Fr. P. about dad's "vision" of Pope Saint John XXIII. Imagine our surprise when Fr. P. told us that he had celebrated Mass for Dad on the tomb of Pope John XXIII. All of us were amazed at this experience of the Communion of Saints. Shortly after that, Dad died peacefully. It was June 23, the eve of the feast of the birth of Saint John the Baptist—the saint who had leapt in the womb when Mary came to help his mother, Elizabeth. In some mysterious way, the holy Pope was connected with the Baptist and with Mary. It was beautiful to know that my

father had these heavenly patrons to lead him to eternal life.

Isn't that amazing? They didn't even know that this priest had celebrated Mass on the tomb of John XXIII until afterward. But it's not unusual for people who are dying to see a saint or the Blessed Mother, who comes to help them enter eternity. The saints can help us in practical ways like this. Although the bodies of the saints will not be raised until the end of time, God can allow a vision like this to help us when we need it.

Mary assumed into heaven is a sign that gives us hope. It reminds us of our own destiny—eternal life with God. When we are going through difficult times, it helps to remember that these will pass soon enough, and that we are destined for eternal happiness in heaven. Of all the trials we may endure in our lives, the death of loved ones can be the most difficult. The loss of a spouse after many years of marriage, the death of a child, a parent, a dear friend, all of these losses can cause great grief. Yet, even in the midst of that sorrow and loss, we know by faith that death is not the final word. As Saint Paul wrote:

> If for this life only we have hoped in Christ, we
> are of all people most to be pitied. But in fact

Christ has been raised from the dead, the first fruits of those who have died. For since death came through a human being, the resurrection of the dead has also come through a human being; for as all die in Adam, so all will be made alive in Christ. But each in his own order: Christ the first fruits, then at his coming those who belong to Christ. Then comes the end, when he hands over the kingdom to God the Father, after he has destroyed every ruler and every authority and power. For he must reign until he has put all his enemies under his feet. The last enemy to be destroyed is death. (1 Cor 15:19–26)

Jesus Christ granted to Mary, his mother, the grace to overcome death in a unique way by her Assumption into heaven. From there, she is always ready to help us by her intercession and prayers. We can turn to her with great trust and confidence, knowing that she is our advocate and help in time of need.

For Reflection and Prayer

1. Does the intercession of Mary and the saints make more sense to you when seen in the context of the Church as the Body of Christ?

2. Have there been times in your own life when you feel you have been helped by the prayers of others?

3. How does the hope of eternal life sustain you in times of difficulty?

Walking with Mary

"Mary brought and brings to the Church the greatest fruit of salvation and always new outpourings of the Holy Spirit."

"Mary has boundless care and solicitude for each of her children. . . . That is why we should confide in this mother."

BLESSED JAMES ALBERIONE

The following stories are true accounts from people who believe they were helped through Mary's intercession. Some stories also reflect ways in which the persons concerned have grown in their devotion to Mary. While such accounts are not matters of faith, they can remind us of the variety of ways in which Mary aids us through her intercession. Catholics have always honored Mary and invoked her help in times of need.

Sister Martha, Louisiana

It was 1982 and I was twenty-two years old. I had just returned to the deep South after working in fast-paced Manhattan. I was also a "junior nun," having made my first vows just six months earlier. I certainly had a lot to learn! Adjusting to life as a professed sister was no small feat, and I kept running into obstacles. I had to tangle with everyone's expectations, mine being the highest. I thought that once I had made my first vows, I could just work hard and reach the perfection of love easily with God's help. Right? Wrong! God wanted to teach me many things, humility first of all. My plans did not seem to coincide with God's. So I struggled, worried, and found myself quite disheartened at my many failures. At times I was totally engulfed in a major bout of scrupulosity. It was exhausting. Who kept me sane through all this? Mary. The organist at our parish, a Salesian named Sister Patricia, used to play a sort of lilting march-type hymn, "Remember, Virgin Mary, that never was it known . . ." and I would sing it and pray it when I was especially down. I could feel Mary supporting me and helping me. I can look back and see clearly how she was encouraging me, helping me to keep on trusting in the Lord. Ever since then, the Memorare has been my favorite prayer. (See the selection of prayers toward the end of this book.) I pray it often, confident that "*never* was it known that *anyone* who fled to your protection . . . has been left unaided!" Mary was faithful to me and supported me in my "Yes." Today, after more than thirty years as a Daughter of St. Paul, I rejoice in her consistent, loving presence. She keeps me walking on my journey to God.

Madonna Janet K., California

When my mother was in her thirties, her own mother died unexpectedly. One of the dreams that my grandmother had shared with my Mom was that of making a pilgrimage to Lourdes, but she never had the opportunity.

Grandmother left Mom a small legacy, just enough for her, my Dad, and my three-year-old brother, Stephen, who had been born with spinal bifida, to travel from our home in Hawaii to Lourdes. Mom was asking Mary for special graces and help for Stephen—that he would be able to walk and to thrive.

After arriving in Lourdes, my Mom was troubled with second thoughts about using the funds on this trip when our family, with five other children at that time, was struggling financially.

During the candlelight procession one night, Mom was on one of the bridges overlooking the crowds in procession. She distinctly heard from behind her the sound of her mother's voice singing "Immaculate Mary" along with all the pilgrims. Mom knew then that her mother was there with her and was rejoicing that she had come to Lourdes.

The graces Mom asked for Stephen from Mary were also granted. Although he wasn't fully cured, he has been able to walk—first with braces and then a cane—and he certainly thrives and is close to Mary. I also know that Mary strengthened my Mom's own faith, which she faithfully practiced all her life. Mom's last prayer when she died at the age of eighty-eight was the Rosary.

Jackie H., New York

I have no doubt that Mary has helped me in many ways that I don't even realize. However, I have one special story that I can attribute directly to her.

I had just graduated from college and had gotten my first job at a tech company. One day I brought in some leftover spaghetti to heat in the microwave for my lunch. As I pulled the plate out, the burning hot spaghetti slid right off the plate onto my arms, then on the floor. I was in terrible pain since my arm was badly burned. After putting on an ice compress, I was excused from work. I didn't seek medical attention since it didn't blister, and I thought the cold compress would be enough. Still, I could only bear the searing pain with the compress on my arm.

That night I was still in the same sorry condition and lay down in bed with my arm bent over into an ice bucket. This was quite uncomfortable, and I thought that the pain would awaken me when the ice water got warm. I said my prayers, asking Mary to stop the pain and heal my arm so I could sleep. I was very tired and couldn't keep my eyes open at that point except for the pain in my arm. I ended my prayer, and suddenly, as if someone had flipped a switch, the pain ceased. I whispered my thank you, put the bucket down, and fell asleep. I know that it was Mary who made the burning pain stop instantly. It was the most direct intervention of Mary that I am aware of in my own life. What a good loving Mother we have!

SISTER SUSAN JAMES, MASSACHUSETTS

In 2004, as I celebrated my twenty-fifth anniversary of religious profession, I was blessed to make a thirty-day Ignatian retreat. With the help of a wise director, I navigated the various segments of the retreat, praying with the life of Christ and the various Gospel scenes. Everything was progressing fairly smoothly until I was meditating on the call of the disciples and began to experience difficulty.

As a religious of an active-contemplative community, I felt that I should be able to connect with Jesus's invitation to Peter, James, and John. I tried to picture the scene: the boats, the nets, and the call to be fishers of men, but nothing stirred or moved my heart. I felt confused. After several hours of praying, I sat quietly before Jesus in the Blessed Sacrament waiting and wondering how I could continue.

Then I received a special grace, one I later realized was the pivotal grace of the retreat. The Lord inwardly spoke to my heart saying: "You need to look to Mary to understand your role." These simple words gave so much illumination and direction. Mary was the Dwelling Place and God-Bearer, the woman of discernment who understood God's timing, the woman of faith and courage at the foot of the cross, lover of the Body of Christ (the Church). This invitation guided the rest of my retreat and still guides my busy apostolic life.

"Look to Mary" I was told, and, like her, love Christ in his Body the Church, be a woman of courage and mature faith. Be a serene presence filled with the divine indwelling and beseech the abundant outpouring of the Holy Spirit on the Church and in the world. My life as a sister is to be patterned after that of Mary, Mother of Christ, Mother of the Apostles, Mother of the Church. I pray to live this wonderful vocation in her company and following her lead.

ANONYMOUS

For some years I had a disagreement with my brother regarding the settlement of my parents' will. It was a painful disagreement because it caused a break in my relationship with my brother. It was a complicated situation and both of us suffered a great deal with the estrangement that we felt. I continued to send cards and notes and tried my best to keep in contact with him. I finally prayed the thirty-day Rosary novena for the intention of reconciliation with him. A short time later he called and we were able to clarify the situation and explain our views with respect. I am very grateful to Mary for her intercession in this painful situation. Today my brother and I are very close and supportive of one another. I am sure that Mary's intercession helped to heal the relationship.

Margaret K., Louisiana

This event took place around 1965 in Louisiana. Our good friends and neighbors, who were Mexican-American, were moving to Arkansas from Louisiana. They planned to drive in two cars. It was a time of unrest in the South, with the civil rights movement in full swing. Every day brought news of such events as Martin Luther King's march and the march from Selma to Montgomery, Alabama. Even though our neighbors followed each other out of Louisiana, their cars became separated. John drove back to our house because he didn't know where else to turn. He told my mom and dad that they lost track of his wife, Nancy, and their youngest child, just a baby, as both cars drove out of Louisiana.

The first thing Mom did was light a candle, and we all knelt down to pray the Rosary. Our friends were not Catholic, but Mom's conviction that Mary would unite the family was so strong that we all began to pray. In the middle of the Rosary Nancy rang the front door bell! She said that she had lost John and didn't know where else to go. The joy in our house was immense! Mom reminded us to finish the Rosary in thanksgiving, and we did.

CHRISTINE, CALIFORNIA

Safety. Warmth. Love. These feelings arise spontaneously when I think of the Blessed Virgin Mary. When I do so, her Son, Jesus, is almost always a part of the thought in some way. He is the center of our relationship. I did not always understand it as such. I was born into a Catholic family, attended Catholic school, and was part of a couple of Marian groups in school and at our parish. Despite this, for a long time relating to Mary was a struggle for me. I often felt that my relationship with Mary took away from my relationship with Jesus. I wanted to love Jesus with all my heart, with all my soul, and with my strength. I also wanted to love and honor his mother who is also my mother—our mother. With time and continuous prayers to Mary about this and other needs, I realized that there was no conflict and there never had been. I gradually began to experience the truth of the words: "To Jesus through Mary." I realized that despite my struggle Mary had been (and continues to be) a gentle presence in my life, quietly leading me to Jesus and helping me to listen to him. When I pray the Rosary or just simply talk to her, I am reminded of her words: *Do whatever he tells you.*

Peter Z., Canada

My father was very connected to our holy Mother Mary, and although he made sure that he taught me about all aspects of our faith, he always told me to pray extra hard to Our Lady! When I was a young boy, he took me to Saint Bruno, Quebec, because two children said Our Lady appeared to them. There was no return visit by Mary on the day the children had claimed she would return, but that didn't matter to my father. I think it meant so much more to him to be a part of a large group of people who loved Our Lady as much as he did. That day is as clear as ever for me.

My connection to Mother Mary was permanently sealed into my heart when I went to Lourdes, France, when I was twenty-one. The daily processions and immersion of the sick in the anointed baths opened up my soul like it had never been opened before. It was then that I believe the gift of faith entered my soul forever. I'm fifty now and, despite experiencing hard times in my life again, I never feel alone or forgotten.

Sister Mary Joseph, Massachusetts

Once when I felt the need and desire to renew my devotion to Mary, she came to me in my prayer. At her initiative, she came and sat beside me, to be near me as a friend to encourage and strengthen me. I had been reflecting on one of the hard sayings of Jesus and imagined applying it to myself. How humbling when my conscience was aware of all my failings. Yet knowing and believing that God loves us in our nothingness, I tried to feel that love. In the midst of it Mary came to sit beside me as sister, as friend, as another woman, with knowing and caring tenderness and understanding. I felt that she was with me.

As I pondered what "devotion" to do or follow in Mary's honor, it became clear: to be to others what she was to me. That is, to be "with" others as a sister, a friend, in order to support others. That's how I could be like Mary and honor her, for imitation is, after all, the highest form of admiration and of honoring someone.

DIANE K., CALIFORNIA

When I was growing up, we used to gather after supper in the living room as a family to pray the Rosary together. To make it more meaningful and to give us a prayerful atmosphere, my parents got a statue of Mary. Mom and Dad took us to the Daughters of St. Paul Catholic book store and we picked out a lovely, colorful statue of the Blessed Mother. We placed this in the living room along with one or two small glass vigil candles. So, before beginning the Rosary, the atmosphere was set by lighting the candles and gathering near the statue of Mary. From my parents' example, I grew to love the Rosary and the Blessed Mother, thinking of the scenes in the lives of Jesus and Mary.

I remember a very strong moment of need when we turned to Mary in a special way: Mom was pregnant and became critically ill. An ambulance rushed her to the hospital, and Dad went with her. My older sister and I (we were about thirteen and

eleven years old) knelt down that morning in front
of the Blessed Mother statue and prayed the
Rosary, asking Mary to intercede. Because of the
serious situation, we knew the best thing to do was
ask Mary for her help. Our Mom had an emer-
gency C-section delivery of our little brother, John,
who was immediately baptized since he was prema-
ture. The doctors did what they could, but his lungs
were not fully developed and he only lived eight
hours. Although Mom had been in critical condition, she survived with very few complications. I
feel Mary brought her through for us, and we have
a little brother saint in heaven. I love the Rosary and
feel it is a powerful and a contemplative prayer that
brings with it many graces for following Jesus and
Mary more closely in our lives.

DENISE B., MASSACHUSETTS

A few years ago, my Mom passed away suddenly. It was a difficult time for me, for we had been
very close. Moreover, there had not been any time
to say goodbye. In the following days, I experienced
not only the deep pain of grief, but a stark empti-
ness. My Mom was gone, and I felt very alone. One
day, as I was helping to clean her apartment, I
found her rosary tucked into the side pocket of the

recliner. That night, as I prayed the Rosary, I held her beads in my hands. All of a sudden, a powerful feeling of Mary's presence came over me, and I felt cradled like a child in her arms. And there, with Mary holding me, I sensed the presence of my Mom. This brought tears to my eyes, peace to my mind, and comfort to my heart. It was almost as though Our Lady was telling me that she, my mother, is with me, but that my Mom is still with me too.

Now, every time I pray the Rosary, I remember that moment, and I remember that Mary is very close to me—and so is my Mom. The Rosary gives me strength and courage and reminds me every day that Mary will never leave me, and neither will my Mom.

ANNE, NEW YORK

I had often worn a Miraculous Medal as a sign of devotion to Mary. Over time, however, it became something I was putting on in the morning without much thought. Then one day I noticed that a Marian wall calendar in my room featured the prayer of consecration to Our Lady of the Miraculous Medal. I remembered this prayer from having prayed the novena at my parish church when

I was young. So I began to say this prayer each day
as I put on the medal. By renewing my dedication
to Mary every morning, the medal became more
meaningful to me. It became what a sacramental is
truly meant to be: a sign of God's presence and, in
this case, a reminder of Mary's loving protection, as
the prayer says: "May this medal be for each one of
us a sure sign of your affection for us and a constant reminder of our duties toward you. Ever while
wearing it, may we be blessed by your loving protection and preserved in the grace of your Son."

SISTER CHRISTINE, PENNSYLVANIA

I was baptized a Catholic as a baby but grew up
in an un-churched home. I had no catechetical formation, and I knew only the barest essentials about
Jesus. When I was twelve years old I read a book
that touched me. It was Franz Werfel's *The Song of
Bernadette*. I was very attracted to the Catholic faith
and especially to Mary. The beautiful dialogue of
Mary with Saint Bernadette impressed me, especially when Mary asked, "Will you do me the favor
of coming here . . . ?" It was such a respectful and
delicate question from God's mother to a simple
French girl. The powerful story of Our Lady of
Lourdes and Saint Bernadette drew me into the

Catholic faith and ultimately to my religious vocation.

I can honestly say that I owe my faith and vocation to Franz Werfel, a devout Jew, who promised to sing the "Song of Bernadette" to the world if he and his wife were spared from the Nazis.

ANONYMOUS

One year I had the wonderful grace to go on a pilgrimage to Lourdes. Surrounded by devoted pilgrims, I was embarrassed for my lack of fervor. Spiritually I felt as cold as the rock on which the Immaculate Virgin Mary appeared to Saint Bernadette. I prayed that the privilege of being there would not be fruitless for me. My prayer was answered when I visited the first chapel that had been built there. With my eyes on the tabernacle, my heart heard Mary say: "Here I am, with my Son."

Devotions and Prayers

"Mary is the perfect Orans (pray-er), a figure of
the Church. . . . The prayer of the Church is sustained
by the prayer of Mary and united with it in hope."

Catechism of the Catholic Church, no. 2679

BASIC MARIAN PRAYERS

The Oldest Prayer to Mary

In 1917, a third-century Egyptian papyrus was discovered with the text of this prayer. It is the oldest known prayer asking Mary's intercession. The Latin version begins with the words "Sub tuum praesidium."

We fly to your protection,
O holy Mother of God;
despise not our petitions in our necessities,
but deliver us always from all dangers,
O glorious and blessed Virgin.
Amen.

The Hail Mary

The Hail Mary is the most popular and well-known Marian prayer. It is drawn from the Gospel—from the Angel Gabriel's words to

Mary at the annunciation, and from Saint Elizabeth's greeting to Our Lady.

Hail Mary, full of grace, the Lord is with you, blessed are you among women, and blessed is the fruit of your womb, Jesus.
Holy Mary, Mother of God, pray for us sinners, now and at the hour of our death. Amen.

The Angelus

Customarily prayed at morning, noon, and evening, the Angelus prayer is a way to dedicate our entire day to God through the intercession of Mary.

The angel of the Lord declared unto Mary.
And she conceived of the Holy Spirit.

Hail Mary, full of grace, the Lord is with you,
blessed are you among women,
and blessed is the fruit of your womb, Jesus.
Holy Mary, Mother of God, pray for us sinners,
now and at the hour of our death. Amen.

Behold the handmaid of the Lord,
be it done unto me according to your word.
Hail Mary....

And the Word was made flesh.
And dwelt among us.
Hail Mary....

Pray for us, O Holy Mother of God, that we may be made worthy of the promises of Christ.

Let us pray:

Pour forth, we beseech you, O Lord, your grace into our hearts, that we, to whom the Incarnation of Christ, your Son, was made known by the message of an angel, may by his passion and cross be brought to the glory of his resurrection, through the same Christ our Lord. Amen.*

The Regina Caeli (Queen of Heaven)

During the Easter season, the Regina Caeli is prayed in place of the Angelus.

Queen of heaven, rejoice, alleluia:
For he whom you merited to bear, alleluia,
Has risen, as he said, alleluia.

---

* See "The Angelus Project" by Sister Anne Joan Flanagan for a beautiful video presentation of how to pray the Angelus: http://calltoprayer.blogspot.com/.

Pray for us to God, alleluia.
Rejoice and be glad, O Virgin Mary, alleluia.
For the Lord has truly risen, alleluia.

Let us pray: O God, who by the resurrection of your Son, our Lord Jesus Christ, has been pleased to fill the world with joy, grant, we beseech you, that through the intercession of the Virgin Mary, his Mother, we may receive the joys of eternal life, through the same Christ our Lord. Amen.

Hail, Holy Queen

*H*ail, holy Queen, Mother of mercy, our life, our sweetness, and our hope! To you we cry, poor banished children of Eve; to you we send up our sighs, mourning and weeping in this valley of tears. Turn then, most gracious advocate, your eyes of mercy toward us, and after this our exile, show unto us the blessed fruit of your womb, Jesus. O clement, O loving, O sweet Virgin Mary.

Memorare

Remember, O most gracious Virgin Mary, that never was it known that anyone who fled to your protection, implored your help, or sought your intercession was left unaided. Inspired with this confidence, I fly to you, O Virgin of virgins, my Mother; to you I come; before you I stand, sinful and sorrowful. O Mother of the Word Incarnate, despise not my petitions, but in your mercy hear and answer them. Amen.

VARIOUS MARIAN PRAYERS AND DEVOTIONS

Loving Mother of the Redeemer

Loving Mother of the Redeemer,
gate of heaven, star of the sea,
assist your people who have fallen,
yet strive to rise again.
To the wonderment of nature
you bore your Creator,
yet remained a virgin after as before.
You who received Gabriel's joyful greeting,
have pity on us poor sinners.

Attributed to Blessed Herman the Lame

Prayer for the Ministers of the Word

O Mary,
you who gave birth
to the Word made flesh,
be present among us:

assist, inspire, and comfort
the ministers of the Word.

O Mary,
you who are the Queen of Apostles,
intervene with your protection
that the light of the Gospel
may reach all peoples.

O Mary,
Mother of Jesus, Way, Truth, and Life,
intercede for us
so that heaven may be filled
with those who sing the hymn of glory
to the Most Holy Trinity.

By Blessed James Alberione, SSP

THE ROSARY

How to Pray the Rosary

The complete Rosary consists of four sets of mysteries, each containing five decades: the Joyful Mysteries, which are ordinarily prayed on Mondays and Saturdays; the Luminous Mysteries, prayed on Thursdays; the Sorrowful Mysteries, which are prayed on Tuesdays and Fridays; and the Glorious Mysteries, usually prayed on Wednesdays and Sundays.

To pray the Rosary as the blend of contemplative and vocal prayer that it is meant to be, it is recommended to meditate on the individual mysteries while reciting the prayers. In this way, the Rosary will bring us closer to Jesus and Mary and help us grow in our Christian life.

We begin the Rosary by blessing ourselves with the crucifix. Then we may recite the Apostles' Creed, one Our Father, three Hail Marys, and one Glory to the Father on the small chain. Then we pray one Our Father, ten Hail Marys, and one Glory to the Father. This completes one decade, and all the other decades are recited in the same manner with a different mystery meditated during each decade. At the end of the Rosary, the Hail Holy Queen and the Litany of the Blessed Virgin may be recited.

The Mysteries of the Rosary

Joyful Mysteries

1. The Annunciation to the Blessed Virgin Mary
2. Mary Visits Her Cousin Elizabeth
3. The Birth of Jesus at Bethlehem
4. The Presentation of Jesus in the Temple
5. The Finding of the Child Jesus in the Temple

Luminous Mysteries

1. John Baptizes Jesus in the Jordan
2. Jesus Reveals His Glory at the Wedding of Cana
3. Jesus Proclaims the Kingdom of God and Calls Us to Conversion
4. The Transfiguration of Jesus
5. Jesus Gives Us the Eucharist

Sorrowful Mysteries

1. Jesus Prays in the Garden of Gethsemani
2. Jesus Is Scourged at the Pillar
3. Jesus Is Crowned with Thorns
4. Jesus Carries the Cross to Calvary
5. Jesus Dies for Our Sins

Glorious Mysteries

1. Jesus Rises from the Dead
2. Jesus Ascends into Heaven
3. The Holy Spirit Descends on the Apostles
4. Mary Is Assumed into Heaven
5. Mary is Crowned Queen of Heaven and Earth

Litany of the Blessed Virgin Mary (Litany of Loreto)

This ancient litany goes back to the early sixteenth century, and in 1587 Pope Sixtus V officially approved its use. It was popular at the Shrine of Our Lady of Loreto, Italy. In 1995 Pope John Paul II added the title, "Queen of Families."

V. Lord, have mercy.
R. *Christ have mercy.*

V. Lord have mercy. Christ hear us.

R. Christ graciously hear us.

God the Father of heaven,	*have mercy on us.*
God the Son, Redeemer of the world,	*have mercy on us.*
God the Holy Spirit,	*have mercy on us.*
Holy Trinity, one God,	*have mercy on us.*
Holy Mary,	*pray for us.*
Holy Mother of God,	*pray for us.*
Holy Virgin of Virgins,	*pray for us.*
Mother of Christ,	*pray for us.*
Mother of divine grace,	*pray for us.*
Mother most pure,	*pray for us.*
Mother most chaste,	*pray for us.*
Mother inviolate,	*pray for us.*
Mother undefiled,	*pray for us.*
Mother most amiable,	*pray for us.*
Mother most admirable,	*pray for us.*
Mother of Good Counsel,	*pray for us.*
Mother of our Creator,	*pray for us.*
Mother of our Savior,	*pray for us.*
Virgin most prudent,	*pray for us.*
Virgin most venerable,	*pray for us.*
Virgin most renowned,	*pray for us.*
Virgin most powerful,	*pray for us.*
Virgin most merciful,	*pray for us.*

Virgin most faithful,   *pray for us.*

Mirror of justice,   *pray for us.*

Seat of wisdom,   *pray for us.*

Cause of our joy,   *pray for us.*

Spiritual vessel,   *pray for us.*

Vessel of honor,   *pray for us.*

Singular vessel of devotion,   *pray for us.*

Mystical rose,   *pray for us.*

Tower of David,   *pray for us.*

Tower of ivory,   *pray for us.*

House of gold,   *pray for us.*

Ark of the covenant,   *pray for us.*

Gate of heaven,   *pray for us.*

Morning star,   *pray for us.*

Health of the sick,   *pray for us.*

Refuge of sinners,   *pray for us.*

Comforter of the afflicted,   *pray for us.*

Help of Christians,   *pray for us.*

Queen of Angels,   *pray for us.*

Queen of Patriarchs,   *pray for us.*

Queen of Prophets,   *pray for us.*

Queen of Apostles,   *pray for us.*

Queen of Martyrs,   *pray for us.*

Queen of Confessors,   *pray for us.*

Queen of Virgins,   *pray for us.*

Queen of all Saints,   *pray for us.*

Queen conceived without original sin,   *pray for us.*

Queen assumed into heaven,	*pray for us.*
Queen of the most holy Rosary,	*pray for us.*
Queen of families,	*pray for us.*
Queen of peace,	*pray for us.*

V. Lamb of God, Who takes away the sins of the world,

R. *Spare us, O Lord.*

V. Lamb of God, Who takes away the sins of the world,

R. *Graciously hear us, O Lord.*

V. Lamb of God, Who takes away the sins of the world,

R. *Have mercy on us.*

V. Pray for us, O holy Mother of God.

R. *That we may be made worthy of the promises of Christ.*

Let us pray. Grant, we beseech you, O Lord God, that we your servants may enjoy perpetual health of mind and body, and by the glorious intercession of blessed Mary, ever Virgin, may we be freed from present sorrow, and rejoice in eternal happiness. Through Christ our Lord.

R. Amen.

Stabat Mater (Our Lady of Sorrows)

This popular hymn, often recited with the Stations of the Cross, originated in the Middle Ages. One of the few Sequences still used in the Roman Missal, it may be prayed at Mass on the feast of Our Lady of Sorrows (September 15).

At the cross her station keeping,
Stood the mournful Mother weeping,
Close to Jesus to the last.

Through her heart, his sorrow sharing,
All his bitter anguish bearing,
Now at length the sword had passed.

Oh, how sad and sore distressed
Was that Mother highly blessed
Of the sole begotten One!

Christ above in torment hangs,
She beneath beholds the pangs
Of her dying, glorious Son.

Is there one who would not weep,
Whelmed in miseries so deep,
Christ's dear Mother to behold?

Can the human heart refrain
From partaking in her pain,
In that mother's pain untold?

Bruised, derided, cursed, defiled,
She beheld her tender Child,
All with bloody scourges rent.

For the sins of his own nation
Saw him hang in desolation
Till his spirit forth he sent.

O sweet Mother! Font of love,
Touch my spirit from above,
Make my heart with yours accord.

Make me feel as you have felt;
Make my soul to glow and melt
With the love of Christ, my Lord.

Holy Mother, pierce me through,
In my heart each wound renew
Of my Savior crucified.

Let me share with you his pain,
Who for all our sins was slain,
Who for me in torments died.

Let me mingle tears with you,
Mourning him who mourned for me,
All the days that I may live.

By the cross with you to stay,
There with you to weep and pray,
Is all I ask of you to give.

Virgin of all virgins blest!
Listen to my fond request:
Let me share your grief divine.

Let me to my latest breath,
In my body bear the death
Of that dying Son of yours.

Wounded with his every wound,
Steep my soul till it has swooned
In his very Blood away.

Be to me, O Virgin, nigh,
Lest in flames I burn and die,
In his awful judgment day.

Christ, when you shall call me hence,
Be your Mother my defense,
Be your cross my victory.

While my body here decays,
May my soul your goodness praise,
Safe in heaven eternally.
Amen. (Alleluia)

THE SCAPULAR DEVOTION

A scapular usually consists of two pieces of cloth, bearing a religious image, connected with strings and worn over the shoulders. While there are various types of scapulars, the brown scapular is the most popular. It is connected with the feast of Our Lady of Mount Carmel (July 16) and can help us reflect on the biblical theme concerning garments of salvation. The German word for scapular (*Gnadenkleid*) means "grace-garment." Many references to garments and clothes are scattered throughout the Bible, beginning in Genesis: "And the Lord God made garments of skins for the man and for his wife, and clothed them" (Gen 3:21). The need for clothing was an effect of their sin. God's tender action can perhaps be seen as symbolizing the garments of grace that he would bestow through Jesus Christ. Because of their sin, Adam and Eve had to leave the Garden of Eden, and the way to the tree of life was blocked. In the Book of Revelation, we find Jesus has reversed this: "To everyone who conquers, I will give permission to eat from the tree of life that is in the paradise of God" (Rev 2:7), and "Blessed are those who wash their robes [in the blood of the Lamb], so that they will have the right to the tree of life" (Rev 22:14). So wearing a scapular is like expressing in a concrete way that through Baptism we have put on the garments of salvation.

The brown scapular, associated with the Carmelite Order, is meant to help us turn to Mary for protection and help in life's difficulties. It also expresses the reality that our devotion to her is not just something occasional, that we can put on and off as easily as we might put a scapular on and off, but meant to permeate our entire life. It's a sign of the life we live as Christians in following Jesus and striving to grow in holiness.

When putting on one's scapular, it is a good practice to say a prayer such as the following:

The Flower of Carmel

O Beautiful Flower of Carmel, most fruitful vine, splendor of heaven, holy and singular, who brought forth the Son of God, still ever remaining a pure virgin, assist us in our necessity. O Star of the Sea, help and protect us. Show us that you are our Mother. Our Lady of Mount Carmel, pray for us!

Attributed to Saint Simon Stock

THE MIRACULOUS MEDAL

The Miraculous Medal was given by Our Lady to Saint Catherine Labouré, a simple French nun, during apparitions in Paris in 1830. It was distributed widely and due to the graces and favors received through its use, it was given its name.

Prayer of Dedication to Our Lady of the Miraculous Medal

O Virgin Mother of God, Mary Immaculate, we dedicate and consecrate ourselves to you under the title of Our Lady of the Miraculous Medal. May this medal be for each one of us a sure sign of your affection for us and a constant reminder of our duties toward you. Ever while wearing it, may we be blessed by your loving protection and preserved in the grace of your Son. O Most Powerful Virgin, Mother of our Savior, keep us close to you every moment of our lives. Obtain for us, your children, the grace of a happy death; so that in union with you, we may enjoy the bliss of heaven forever. Amen.

O Mary conceived without sin, pray for us who have recourse to you.

Symbolism of the Medal

The images on the Miraculous Medal contain some important symbolism. On the front side, Mary is portrayed as Saint Catherine Labouré saw her, with her hands outstretched toward us and rays of light streaming from them. This symbolizes the graces she obtains for us through her intercession. She is standing on a globe, with her feet on a serpent, symbolizing her victory over Satan. A scriptural reference for this is the famous text of Genesis 3:15 in which God says to the serpent: "I will put enmity between you and the woman, and between your offspring and hers; he will strike your head, and you will strike his heel."

The prayer, "O Mary, conceived without sin, pray for us who have recourse to you" is inscribed around the edge.

On the reverse side of the medal, a cross appears over the letter "M," and beneath it are two hearts representing the hearts of Jesus and Mary. Twelve stars appear around the edge of the medal, a reference to the text of Revelation 12:1 that is often applied to Mary: "A great portent appeared in heaven: a woman clothed with the sun, with the moon under her feet, and on her head a crown of twelve stars."

Cardinal Newman's Prayer in Honor of Our Lady

O Mother of Jesus and my Mother, let me dwell with you, cling to you, and love you with ever-increasing love. I promise the honor, love, and trust of a child. Give me a mother's protection. I need your watchful care. You know better than any other the thoughts and desires of the Sacred Heart of Jesus. Keep constantly before my mind the same thoughts, the same desires, that my heart may be filled with zeal for the interests of the Sacred Heart of your divine Son. Instill in me a love of all that is noble, that I may no longer be easily roused to resentment, easily let to anger, or easily turned to selfishness.

Help me, dearest Mother, to acquire the virtues that God wants of me: to forget myself always, to work solely for him, without fear of sacrifice. I shall always rely on your help to be what Jesus wants me to be. I am his; I am yours, my good Mother! Give me each day your holy and maternal blessing until my last evening on earth, when your Immaculate Heart will present me to the Heart of Jesus in heaven, there to love and bless you and your divine Son for all eternity.

BLESSED JOHN HENRY NEWMAN

DEVOTION OF
THE FIVE FIRST SATURDAYS

Honoring Mary on Saturday is a long-standing Catholic tradition. As a result of the Marian apparitions at Fatima, we have a special devotion known as the Five First Saturdays. On December 10, 1925, the Blessed Virgin appeared to Lucia (one of the Fatima visionaries) who was then a postulant in Spain. Mary told her:

"Look, my daughter, at my heart encircled with thorns, with which ungrateful men wound it every moment by their blasphemies and ingratitude. Give me consolation, you, at least; and announce for me that I promise to assist at the hour of death, with the graces necessary for salvation, all who on the first Saturday of five consecutive months confess, receive Holy Communion, recite five decades of the Rosary, and keep me company for fifteen minutes meditating on the mysteries of the Rosary, with the purpose of making reparation to me."

Offering reparation to Mary's Immaculate Heart is the unique aspect of this devotion. Mary's promise of obtaining special graces for salvation presupposes that the person who offers this devotion intends to live a holy life. The conditions for obtaining this promise are that on the first Saturday of five consecutive months, in a spirit of reparation the person:

1. Receives Holy Communion
2. Makes a good confession (this can be done a few days before or after the Saturday)
3. Prays five decades of the Rosary, and
4. Meditates for fifteen minutes on the mysteries of the Rosary.

The Three Hail Marys

A very simple devotion is to pray three Hail Marys at the end of the day. This is an ancient practice, recommended by saints such as Anthony of Padua, Leonard of Port Maurice, and Alphonsus de Liguori. Because it is short and easy to do, no matter how tired one might be, it is a simple way to honor Mary and ask her to keep us free from sin.

DEVOTION TO MARY,
UNTIER OF KNOTS

This devotion, although not well-known, is becoming more popular because Pope Francis has been promoting it. When he was a Jesuit priest studying in Germany, he came across a beautiful painting of Mary that impressed him deeply. The painting portrays an angel giving Mary a long cord full of knots. Patiently, the Virgin is undoing the knots and straightening out the cord. This symbolism reflects a deeper spiritual reality, that Mary can help us get out of the various tangles and complicated situations we weave in our lives.

The devotion is actually based on a long-standing comparison of Mary with Eve. Saint Irenaeus, an early Church writer, wrote during the second century, "The knot of Eve's disobedience was loosed by the obedience of Mary. For what the virgin Eve had bound fast through unbelief, this did the virgin Mary set free through faith" (*Adversus Haereses*, 3, 22).

Pope Francis wrote the following prayer, which can be prayed as a novena (a prayer or set of prayers repeated for nine days) or whenever desired:

*H*oly Mary, full of God's presence during the
    days of your life,
you accepted with full humility the Father's
    will,
and the Devil was never able to tie you around
    with his confusion
Once with your Son you interceded for our
    difficulties,
and, full of kindness and patience you gave us
    an example of how to untie the knots of
    our life.
By remaining forever our Mother,
you put in order, and make more clear the ties
    that link us to the Lord.
Holy Mother, Mother of God, and our
    Mother,
who untie with a motherly heart the knots of
    our life, we pray to you to receive in your
    hands (the name of person),
and to free him/her of the knots and confu-
    sion with which our enemy attacks.
Through your grace, your intercession, and
    your example,
deliver us from all evil, Our Lady, and untie
    the knots that prevent us from being
    united with God,

so that we, free from sin and error, may find
him in all things, may have our hearts
placed in him, and may serve him always in
our brothers and sisters. Amen.*

---

* For a longer novena, see: http://catholicism.about.com/od/To-Mary-
Undoer-of-Knots/p/Novena-to-Mary-Undoer-of-Knots.htm.

Mary in the Liturgy

SOLEMNITIES

Mary, the Holy Mother of God	January 1
The Annunciation of the Lord	March 25
The Assumption of the Blessed Virgin Mary	August 15
The Immaculate Conception of the Blessed Virgin Mary	December 8

OTHER POPULAR FEASTS

Our Lady of Lourdes	February 11
Our Lady of Fatima	May 13
The Visitation of the Blessed Virgin Mary	May 31
Immaculate Heart of Mary	Saturday after Corpus Christi
Our Lady of Mount Carmel	July 16
Saints Joachim and Anne, parents of the Blessed Virgin Mary	July 26
Dedication of the Basilica of Saint Mary Major	August 5

The Queenship of the Blessed Virgin Mary	August 22
The Nativity of the Blessed Virgin Mary	September 8
Most Holy Name of Mary	September 12
Our Lady of Sorrows	September 15
Our Lady of the Rosary	October 7
Presentation of the Blessed Virgin Mary	November 21
Our Lady of Guadalupe	December 12

Afterword

Mary, Our Mother, Teacher, and Queen

Mary, you gave life to Jesus, our Savior.
    You are the Mother of God.
I claim you as my Mother, too.
    Lead me always closer to your Son.
Mary, you listened to the Word of God and
    pondered it in your heart.
You grew in wisdom and grace.
Lead me to the school of Jesus, that I may
    know him ever better.
Mary, you gave your life in service to Jesus
    and to Joseph.
Your queenship is one of service.
Teach me to spend my life in loving service
    of God and others. Amen.

Appendix

Marian Consecration

Those who would like to develop their devotion to Mary even more may wish to explore Marian consecration. This practice, recommended by many saints, is a way of binding ourselves to Mary so that she will lead us even closer to Jesus. When we consecrate ourselves to Mary, we offer her our whole life, all that we do and are, and ask her to purify our offering and bring it to Jesus for us. As a young man Saint John Paul II discovered this way of Marian devotion and made it part of his whole life, summed up in his motto *Totus Tuus* (I am all yours).

The following testimony is a powerful example of the difference that this consecration can make in one's life. Since a whole book could be written on this topic alone, the story is followed by some resources for those who would like to find out more.

Mother Forever

Growing up Catholic, I was familiar with Mary in my life. However, in high school I experienced a significant crisis of faith. I was discouraged from practicing my Catholic faith and from praying the Rosary, and momentarily yielded. My parents, enlightened by the Holy Spirit, helped me see that: "I need not change my Catholic faith; I just need to go deeper." During this time of darkness, I asked the Lord to show me the way because I felt lost spiritually. He did this faithfully and granted me the gift of a special guide in my faith journey: our Blessed Mother. Looking back, Mary was always the one looking for me, rather than I for her. I was drawn to pray the Rosary in groups at various stages of my faith journey: in high school, at my local Catholic prayer group, and throughout my graduate school years. These times of prayer were filled with consolation and peace even for one who merely knew *about* Mary. For me, she was still far off, a quick reference point for intercession in time of need.

The life-changing moment in my relationship with the Blessed Mother began after my annual novitiate retreat in July 2012. I experienced many graces and pondered deeply the Lord's invitation to offer myself more wholeheartedly to him as a consecrated religious. In my reflections, however, I asked the Lord how I would learn to become a spouse of Christ. As the retreat ended, I felt that the Lord pointed to his Mother as teacher and guide in my journey of religious consecration and fervent discipleship. I did not know how or when this would happen.

Three months later, I was sent to our convent in New Orleans, Louisiana, for my mission experience for a few months. I had only been there about a month when I learned about a renewed interest in Marian consecration that had been growing among people in the area. They were using the book *33 Days to Morning Glory* by Father Michael Gaitley, MIC. Previously I had made my consecration to Mary using Saint Louis de Montfort's *Total Consecration to Mary* as a guide. However, I would not have envisioned what would take place through this new 33-day retreat on Marian consecration. Built upon the work of Saint Louis de Montfort, I was exposed to embracing Marian consecration anew by looking at the lives of modern day saints (John Paul II, Mother Teresa of Calcutta, and Maximilian Kolbe). I felt encouraged, like Saint John, to invite

Mary into my home (see Jn 19:27) and open myself more completely to her. So I did.

The weeks of the retreat were filled with Mary's presence. I felt her closer to me than ever. She moved from being an acquaintance to a confidant. I felt free to invite her to cook with me, speak through me, and work with me. I could unburden my heart simply to her on life's happenings, and she would shed light for me through people, events, Scripture, and insights. Mary came alive—she was someone whom I could relate to in everyday living! While Scripture may not have many accounts of Mary, her actions and thoughts have become truly worth pondering. The Lord fulfilled his direction of me in pointing to the Blessed Mother as my teacher, guide, and way to learning fervent discipleship. I am forever grateful for the gift of a Mother who is always available, purposefully desires that I encounter her Son more deeply, and to whom I can relay everything. I pray that you, too, may call upon her and invite her into your home. She is well worth it.

Sr. Jacqueline Jean-Marie Gitonga, FSP

Resources

Gaitely, Michael, MIC, *33 Days to Morning Glory* (Stockbridge, MA: Marian Press, 2011).

John Paul II, *Mother of the Redeemer Anniversary Edition* with commentary by M. Jean Frisk (Boston: Pauline Books & Media, 2012).

Trouvé, Marianne Lorraine, FSP (compiler), *A Scriptural Rosary* (Boston: Pauline Books & Media, 2004).

The Mary Page at the University of Dayton: http://campus.udayton.edu/mary/.

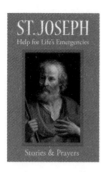

ST. JOSEPH
Help for Life's Emergencies
Compiled and Edited by
Kathryn J. Hermes, FSP

Saint Joseph, foster father of Jesus and husband of Mary, is often called on to intercede in the selling of a house. However, those with a devotion to Saint Joseph know that he can help with much more: employment, family issues, happy death, finances, divine providence, home improvement, and good health. Let the stories and prayers in this book help you open your heart to the care that Saint Joseph can provide.

Paperback	128pp.
#71230	$5.95 U.S.

JESUS
Help in Every Need

Written, Compiled, and Edited by
Kathryn J. Hermes, FSP and
Christine Setticase, FSP

Stories from Scripture, true life experiences and prayers from the Christian tradition draw the reader to look at life from a renewed perspective. In these pages you will be challenged to make changes in your life, your way of thinking and your choices. Allow the Lord's unconditional love and limitless mercy to transform your life.

Paperback   144pp.
#39914 $5.95 U.S.

ANGELS
Help from on High

Written and Compiled by Marianne Lorraine Trouvé, FSP

Who are the angels? Drawing from the official teaching of the Church, popular devotion, and the writings of Saint Thomas Aquinas, this book provides information about the angels. It also contains stories of encountering the angels, and a collection of prayers. Let the prayers and stories of real people who have had help from the angels open your heart to the care they can provide for you.

Paperback   144 pp.
#07907 $5.95 U.S.

BOOKS & MEDIA

A mission of the Daughters of St. Paul

As apostles of Jesus Christ,
evangelizing today's world:

We are CALLED to holiness
by God's living Word and Eucharist.

We COMMUNICATE the Gospel message
through our lives and through all
available forms of media.

We SERVE the Church
by responding to the hopes and needs
of all people with the Word of God,
in the spirit of St. Paul.

For more information visit our website:
www.pauline.org.

BOOKS & MEDIA

The Daughters of St. Paul operate book and media centers at the following addresses. Visit, call or write the one nearest you today, or find us at www.pauline.org

CALIFORNIA
3908 Sepulveda Blvd, Culver City, CA 90230   310-397-8676
935 Brewster Avenue, Redwood City, CA 94063   650-369-4230
5945 Balboa Avenue, San Diego, CA 92111   858-565-9181

FLORIDA
145 S.W. 107th Avenue, Miami, FL 33174   305-559-6715

HAWAII
1143 Bishop Street, Honolulu, HI 96813   808-521-2731
Neighbor Islands call: 866-521-2731

ILLINOIS
172 North Michigan Avenue, Chicago, IL 60601   312-346-4228

LOUISIANA
4403 Veterans Memorial Blvd, Metairie, LA 70006   504-887-7631

MASSACHUSETTS
885 Providence Hwy, Dedham, MA 02026   781-326-5385

MISSOURI
9804 Watson Road, St. Louis, MO 63126   314-965-3512

NEW YORK
64 W. 38th Street, New York, NY 10018   212-754-1110

PENNSYLVANIA
Philadelphia—relocating   215-676-9494

SOUTH CAROLINA
243 King Street, Charleston, SC 29401   843-577-0175

VIRGINIA
1025 King Street, Alexandria, VA 22314   703-549-3806

CANADA
3022 Dufferin Street, Toronto, ON M6B 3T5   416-781-9131

¡También somos su fuente para libros,
videos y música en español!